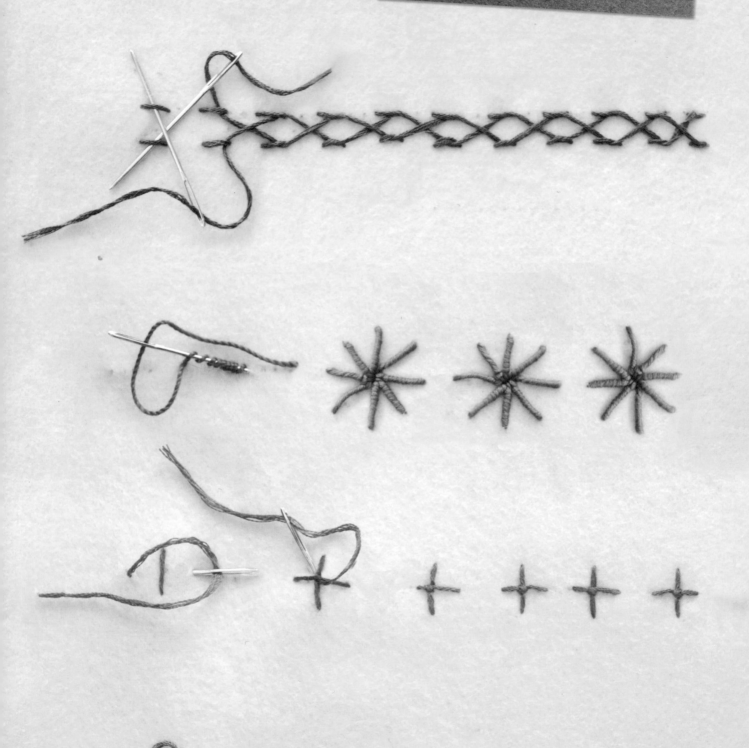

SLIP KNOT
Wrap end over and through the loop and pull tight.

SQUARE KNOT
Wrap two threads and reverse directions for second knot and pull tight.

CROSSED LADDER STITCH – Stitch two rows of running stitches lined up next to each other. Then, with two threaded needles, weave the threads back and forth between the two running stitches creating the ladder effect.

FALSE BULLION STITCH – Make a ½ inch flat stitch, and then from the back, stitch through the first stitch hole. With the needle, wrap floss around the flat stitch 10 times and stitch next to the second flat stitch hole to the back. Repeat the same stitching on the other petals until complete.

FOUR-LEGGED KNOT STITCH – Stitch an X shape using flat stitches. Then, from the back, stitch a tiny anchor edge over the center of the X and back through near where the first thread comes out. Pull tight.

FRENCH KNOT – Stitch from the back, pull the thread tight, and then wind the thread around the needle several times depending on the size of the knot you want. Insert the needle near where the thread comes out, and pull tight.

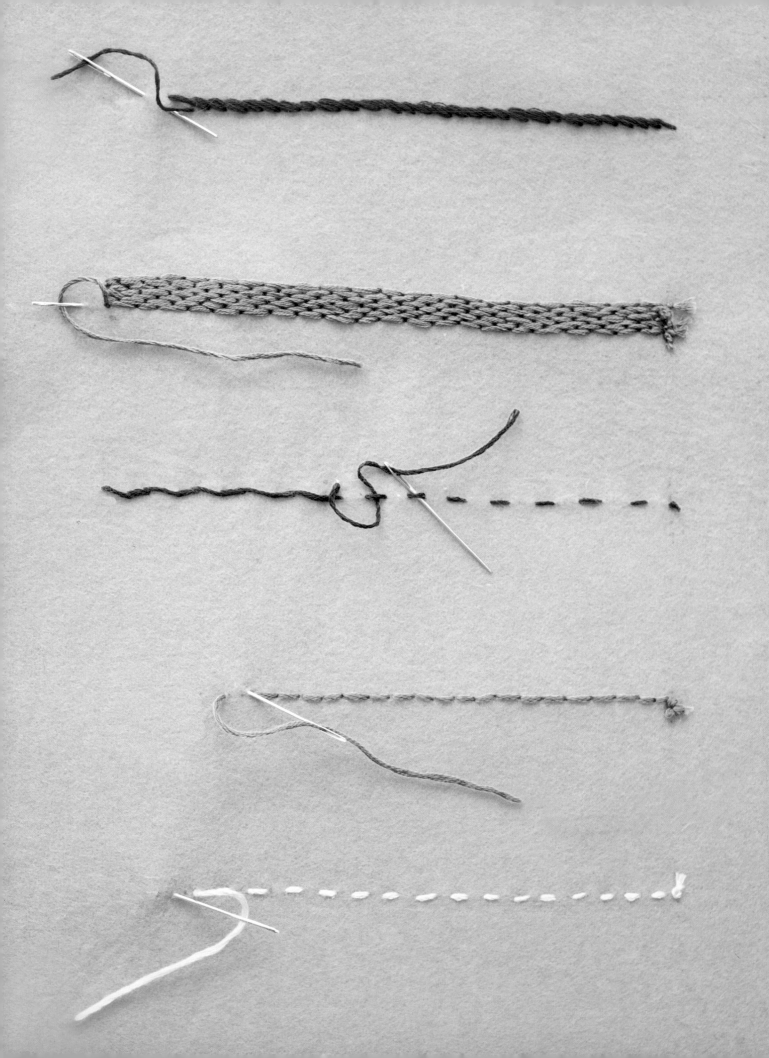

OUTLINE STEM STITCH – Working from left to right, stitch slanted stitches next to each other. Adjusting the angle of the stitch will make thinner or thicker stitch lines.

BRICK STITCH – Make a row of backstitching. Add another row next to it, alternating the starting point to the center point of the previous stitch to create a laid brick look in stitches.

THREADED RUNNING STITCH – Stitch a length of running stitches, and weave under and over through the stitches in a spiral fashion.

BACK STITCH – Make a flat ½ inch stitch. Then, stitching from the back, skip forward one length of a stitch, and stitch back through to the first flat stitch and repeat.

RUNNING STITCH – Make stitches that are equal in size while taking several stitches on the needle at a time.

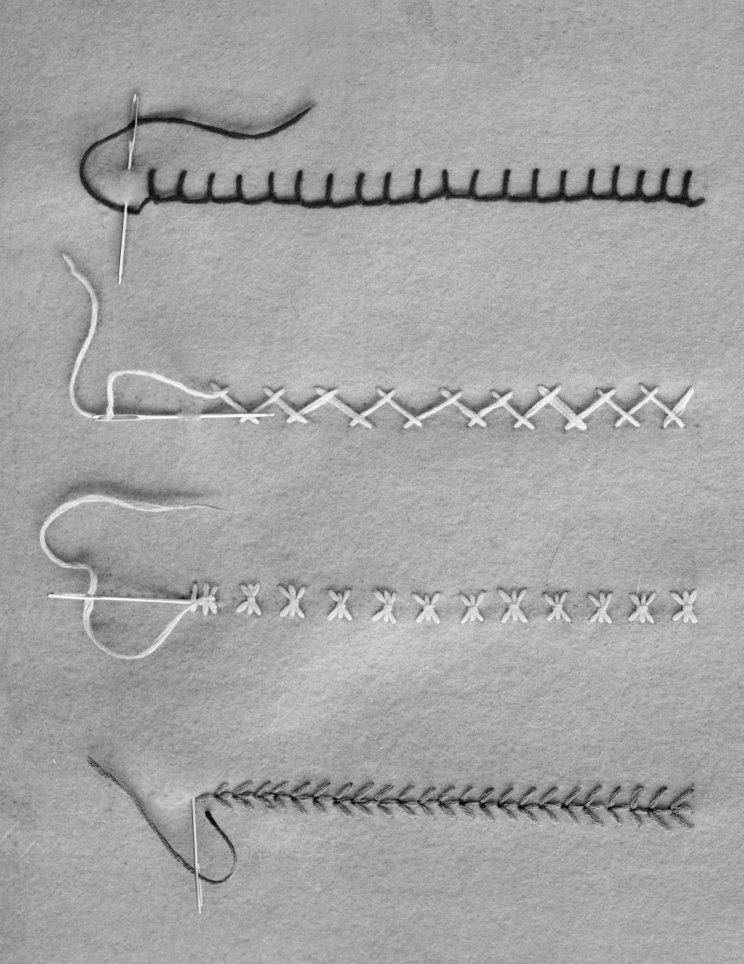

BLANKET STITCH – Make ½ inch stitches, as shown, while wrapping the thread around the needle end and pulling the stitch tight. Repeat.

HERRINGBONE STITCH – Stitch X shapes, starting from the back with flat stitches, but shift the center of the X towards each of the outside edges.

BUNDLE STITCH – Make three ½ inch stitches in a row. Then stitch from the back through to the middle of the center thread and gather all three stitches. Stitch back through the same needle hole.

FERN STITCH – Make a flat stitch and then two angled stitches coming off of the stitch line to create an arrow shape. Repeat.

SLANTED FEATHER STITCH – Make a loose, ½ inch flat stitch going side to side. Stitch from the back ¼ inch forward, centering the stitch between the first two stitch holes. Catch the first stitches loop, and stitch forward ½ inch. Repeat, alternating the sides.

Y STITCH – Make a loose, ½ inch stitch across the fabric. Skip forward ¼ inch, and while centered between the first two stitches, stitch from the back and catch the loose straight stitch. Skip forward ½ inch and stitch to the back, pulling it into a 'Y.' Repeat.

CHAIN STITCH – From the back, stitch through and back through the same hole, leaving a ½ inch loop. Skip forward ¼ inch and stitch to the front, catching the loop and stitching back through the same stitch hole. Repeat.

LAZY DAISY STITCH – Make a stitch from the back and then back through the same hole, leaving a ½ inch loop. From the back, stitch ¼ inch away from the first stitch, catching the end of the loop. Then stitch back through the same hole to secure the petal. Repeat this stitch to a central point to create the flower.

WEB ADDRESS

This overlapping blanket stitching creates a web effect that works well to fill large areas. Start by transferring your design to a fabric. You may stitch along the edge of your design to create a concentric web pattern, or draw a straight line within the design. From there, start stitching to create a grid-like web. Blanket stitch along the transfer line [blanket stitch instructions on page 9]. Start the next row by lining it up with the first, and stitch along the line, matching the stitch holes as you go. Continue stitching until area is filled, and tie off floss on the back. Your embroidery work can be applied to totes, framed artwork, and pillows!

Draw your designs on tracing paper.

1

On the back of the drawing, use a crayon to color over the lines of the drawing. Use a dark color crayon for light fabrics and a light color crayon for dark fabrics.

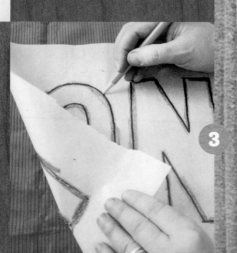

2

Place the design face up on the fabric and re-trace over the design. Be sure to press down firmly on your pencil for best transfer results.

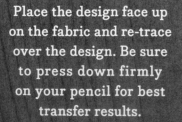

3

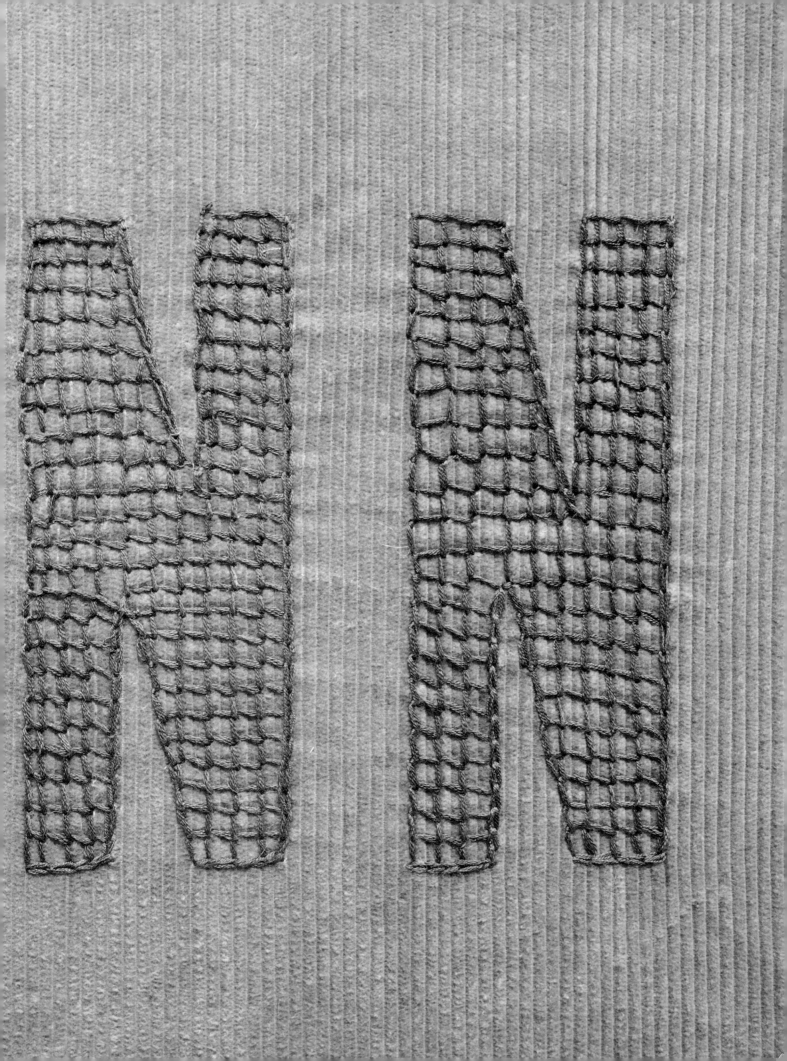

YOU'RE A STAR

Embroider your name or initials in this simple starburst pattern. Make your design, and transfer the pattern to the fabric of your choice. Stitch an X shape centered over the pattern dot. To complete the starburst, repeat stitching four Xs, rotating as you go. Continue stitching over each of your pattern dots until complete. Tie off the floss on the back. This starburst stitch is perfect for embroidering on surfaces where you can't access the back of the fabric, like upholstered furniture or lined clothing.

1 Draw your designs on tracing paper, making marks across it every 1 ½ inch.

2 Puncture at the cross and lay on top of the fabric.

3 Use a marker or pencil to make a small dot on the fabric through the puncture holes.

EMBROIDER-BEE

Get all the buzz on this fast way to transfer designs.

Print out an enlarged photo of a bee, and cut it out.

1

Trace around the outside edges with a marker.

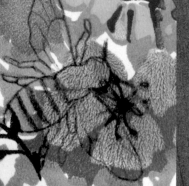

2

Sketch in any prominent details of the bee like the wing forms and stripes.

3

Embroider the bee using a mix of stitches [see pages 4 -11 for stitches ideas]. You can create dimensional designs by layering stitching over stitching. Tie off all threads on the back and iron flat.

4

EMBROIDERY INVASION

Aliens take over! Reconsider the scene by embroidering new motifs and characters onto printed fabrics. This kind of single colored print is called a toile and is the perfect background to start on.

Find a printed fabric with scenes or patterns that is inspiring to embroider over. Use a pencil to sketch the new designs onto the fabric.

1

Use a variety of stitches [see pages 4-11] to execute your designs.

2

Tie off all threads and iron flat. You can stretch your embroidery over a pre-stretched canvas or over a board by stapling or taping the fabric edges onto the back. Frame, or just hang your new artwork, and enjoy!

3

BRIGHT NIGHT OWL

WHO, WHO made this great looking addition to camouflage fabric? YOU DID! Camouflage is a beautiful pattern than can range from abstract shapes in natural colors to realistic scenes of leaves and trees. You can add anything to camouflage patterns; from owls and deer to monsters and graffiti, any combination will look terrific!

1 Transfer your designs in any method you like onto the fabric's face.

2 Select a variety of flosses, from flat cotton to fluffy and hairy yarns.

3 Choose a mix of stitches [see pages 4-11 for ideas] that will be used in your design.

4 Attach an embroidery hoop over the fabric's design. Embroider your design, and tie off all threads on the back.

WILD WEST PLAID

add potent punch to a plaid shirt
by stitching along the lines

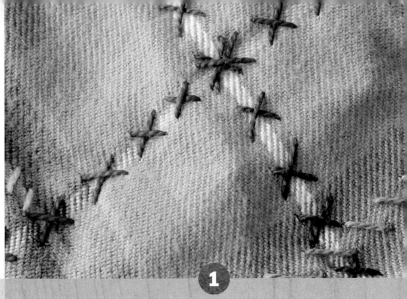

YOU WILL NEED
plaid garment, multi-colored floss, needles, embroidery hoop

Follow along the plaid's lines using a chain stitch. Tie off each thread at the end of the line.

1

2

The decorative whip stitch is a series of ¼ inch diagonal stitches sewn from the back, laid side by side at ⅛ inch intervals to form a line. Use the whip stitch over the top stitching around the armhole.

3

Use a running stitch along the skinnier stripes.

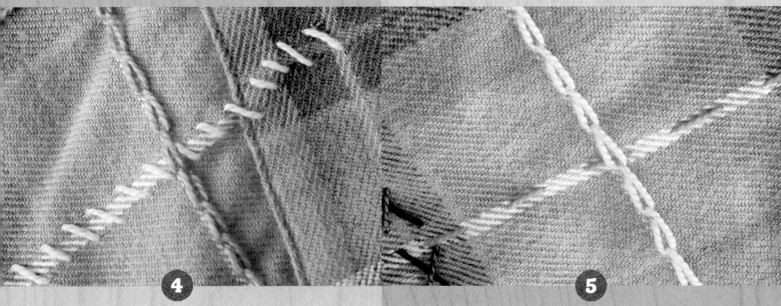

4

On the shirt's back, whip stitch, starting on the yoke towards the bottom of the shirt, for an interesting effect.

5

You can also start and stop cleanly on the stripe, as shown here. When the stitching is finished, press the embroidery and wear proudly!

THREE SWEATER MASH-UP

old, rescued sweaters have never looked better

YOU WILL NEED

cardboard or very heavyweight paper, assorted tapes, glue, scissors, foam brush, decorative papers

1

For a pattern, use a t-shirt that fits you well, but not tight. Fold it in half, and line up the side and bottom on top of one of the sweaters also folded in half. Stick down masking tape along the t-shirt's edge to make a cut line.

2

Cut on the inside edge of the tape as shown, through both sides of sweater.

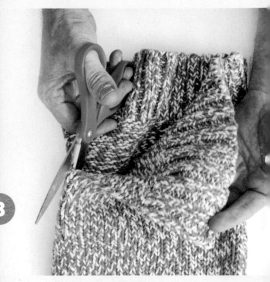

3

Make a single-cut opening through the center, front fold where the zipper will be sewn.

4

This is the new sweater's body shape.

5

To create the sleeves, lay the cut, folded sweater body on top of, and lined up, with the side and shoulder seam of another sweater.

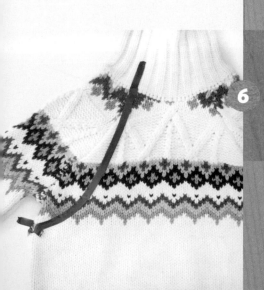

6

Stick down tape, as shown, creating a raglan sleeve.

7

Cut away sleeve, and trim off neck piece. To make the other sleeve, lay the cut sleeve onto the other side of the sweater, and trim around it.

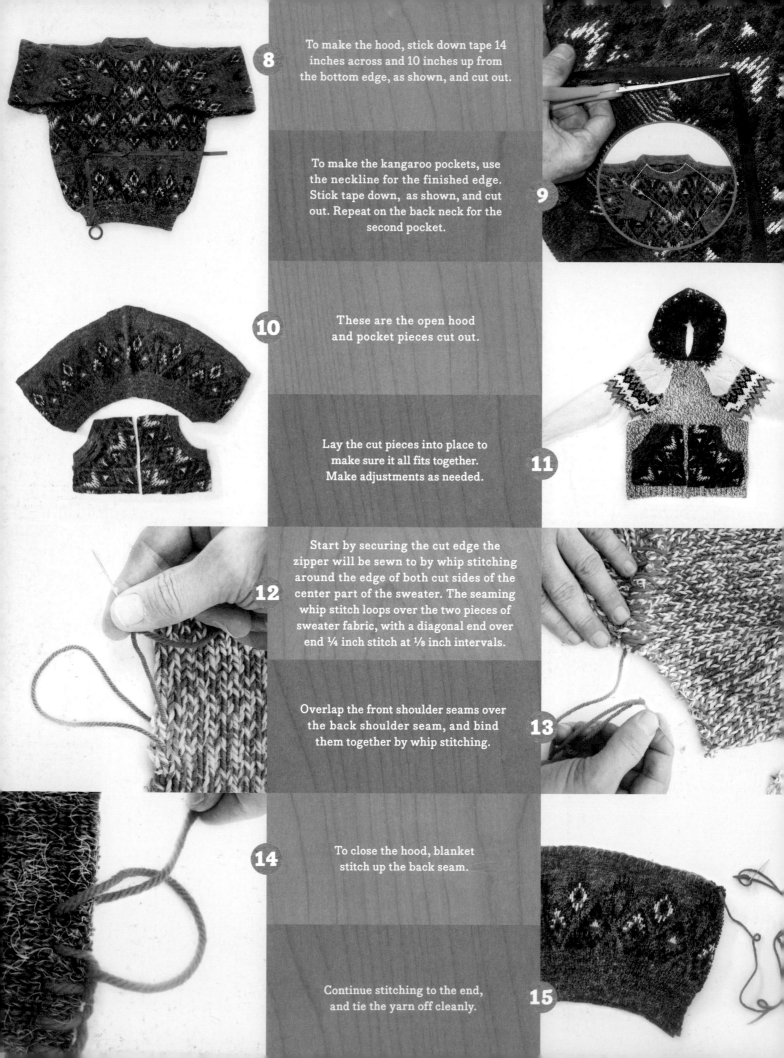

8 To make the hood, stick down tape 14 inches across and 10 inches up from the bottom edge, as shown, and cut out.

9

To make the kangaroo pockets, use the neckline for the finished edge. Stick tape down, as shown, and cut out. Repeat on the back neck for the second pocket.

10 These are the open hood and pocket pieces cut out.

Lay the cut pieces into place to make sure it all fits together. Make adjustments as needed. **11**

12 Start by securing the cut edge the zipper will be sewn to by whip stitching around the edge of both cut sides of the center part of the sweater. The seaming whip stitch loops over the two pieces of sweater fabric, with a diagonal end over end ¼ inch stitch at ⅛ inch intervals.

Overlap the front shoulder seams over the back shoulder seam, and bind them together by whip stitching. **13**

14 To close the hood, blanket stitch up the back seam.

Continue stitching to the end, and tie the yarn off cleanly. **15**

16 Whip stitch the pockets to the front of the body, as shown. Add a few extra stitches around the opening edges of the pocket to secure the pockets.

Attach the second pocket in the same way. **17**

18 Attach the sleeves to the body by whip stitching through the body and the sleeve at the same time.

Line up the center back seam of the hood to the center back of the sweater. **19**

20 Attach the hood by whip stitching it to the body's neck hole. Start stitching toward the front from there, and repeat on the other side.

Lay the zipper on the front, lining up the bottom of the zipper with the sweater bottom. **21**

22 Whip stitch the zipper to the body, as shown.

Fold in any extending zipper at the hood by folding it back and stitching it flat. Press your sweater and enjoy! **23**

SPIDER SPUN STICH

use simple stitches to make a
spooky spider sweatshirt

SUPPLIES

YOU WILL NEED
sweatshirt, cotton floss, needles, ruler, pencil

Draw a straight line from the shoulder to the hem diagonally, and continue drawing Xs, rotating them as you go.

1

2

Draw in the connecting, spiraling draped web lines free hand.

Embroider over the pencil lines using chain stitch, tie off all threads on the back, and press flat when finished.

3

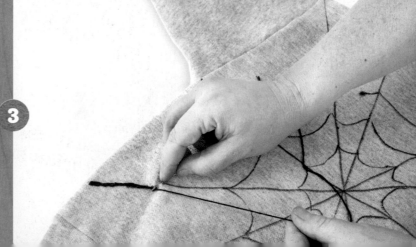

PEGBOARD
PANEL

pre-drilled peg board is a perfect
background for embroidered art